A Helping Hand

Julie Haydon

Contents

A Good Life

We all want to live a good life. A good life means that our needs are met. A good life means that our human rights are protected. A good life means living in peace, not war.

Needs

We need:

- Oxygen, water, food, sleep, and shelter
- Care and love
- Freedom to live the life we want to live

Human Rights

We all have human rights. We are all born free and equal. Things like our **race**, beliefs, **wealth,** or **gender** should not matter.

Some people don't have a good life. Their needs are not met. Their human rights are taken away from them. They do not live in peace.

Some people are very poor.

Some people live in places that have been hit by natural disasters, such as floods or earthquakes.

Some people live in countries that are at war.

Some people are treated unfairly because of their race, beliefs, wealth, or gender.

Some people are punished, or hurt, because of their race, beliefs, wealth, or gender.

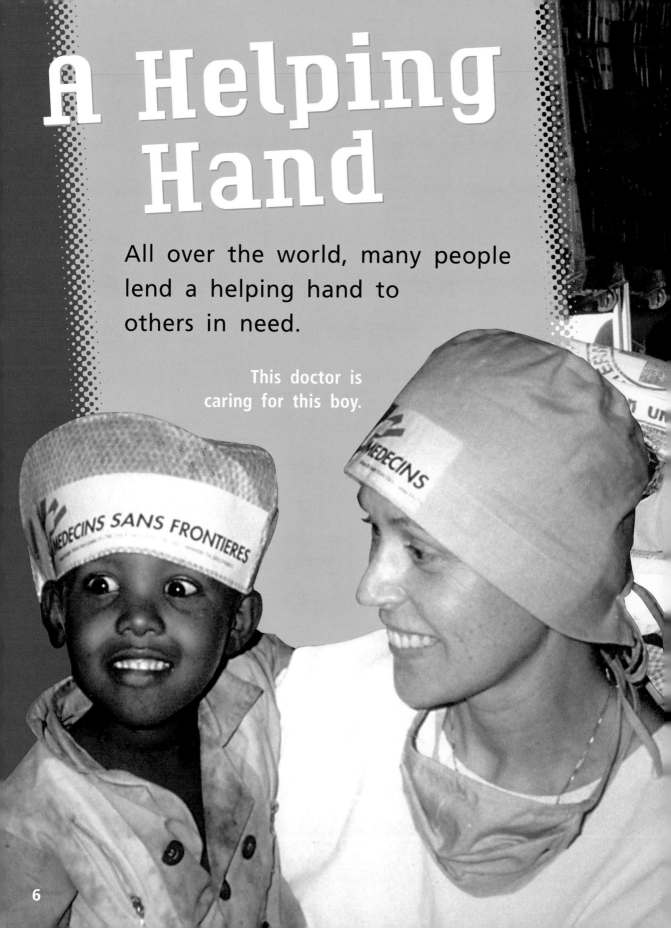

A Helping Hand

All over the world, many people lend a helping hand to others in need.

This doctor is caring for this boy.

Red Cross workers deliver food to people in need.

Help can come from one person, a small group, or a large worldwide organization.

Organizations that help people in need are called humanitarian organizations.

The Red Cross

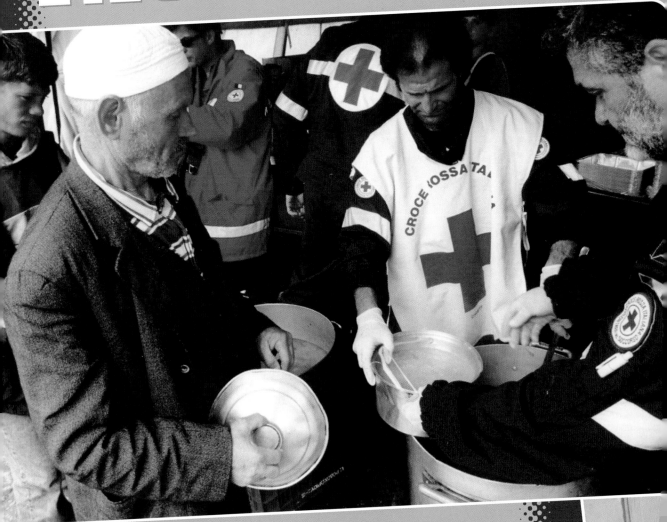

The Red Cross is a worldwide humanitarian organization. It has about 100 million members and **volunteers**.

The Red Cross aims to help all people in need.

What Does the Red Cross Do?

The Red Cross helps and protects victims of natural disasters, wars, and other emergencies. It gives water, food, medical treatment, and shelter to vulnerable people.

What Is the Red Cross Symbol?

The Red Cross symbol is a red cross on a white background.

In some countries, the Red Cross is called the Red Crescent. The symbol is a red moon on a white background.

These symbols mean help!

A symbol must be easy to recognize so that people know what it is and what it means.

Amnesty International

Amnesty International is "a worldwide human rights organization. It has about one million members and volunteers."

The word amnesty means "a pardon or an act of forgiveness, usually granted by a government."

Many people volunteer their services to Amnesty International.

What Does Amnesty International Do?

Amnesty International works to free people who have been jailed because of their race, beliefs, wealth, or gender. It tries to stop prisoners from being treated badly. It also teaches people about human rights.

This volunteer is helping to teach people about human rights.

How Does Amnesty International Work?

Amnesty International members get facts about people who have been jailed unfairly. They write hundreds or thousands of **letters of protest** to governments. They also give information to the media and to the public. Sometimes they conduct **protests**.

What Is the Amnesty International Symbol?

The Amnesty International symbol is a lit candle surrounded by barbed wire.

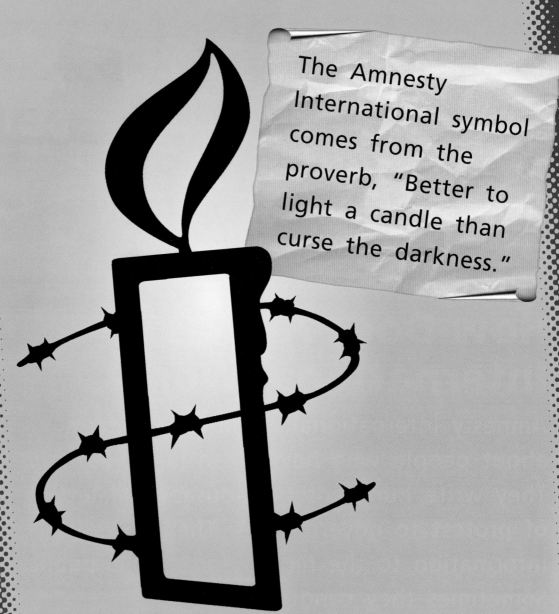

The Amnesty International symbol comes from the proverb, "Better to light a candle than curse the darkness."

Doctors Without Borders

Doctors Without Borders is a worldwide humanitarian organization. It has over 2,500 volunteers. Most of them are doctors and health workers.

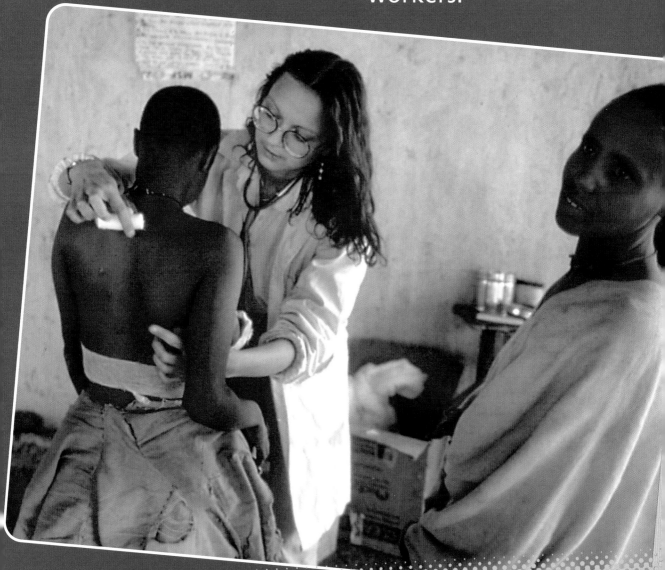

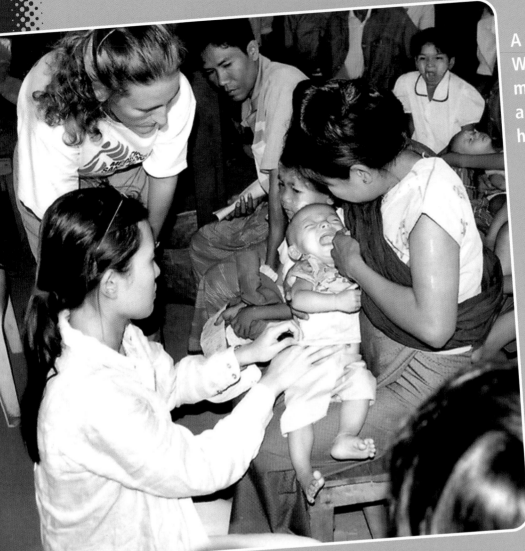

What Does Doctors Without Borders Do?

Doctors Without Borders members help victims of natural disasters and wars. They feed people during **famines**. They fight diseases and set up health centers in poor countries.

Does Doctors Without Borders Have a Symbol?

Doctors Without Borders has a symbol of a volunteer crossing a country's border to give medical care. This organization was started in France. Its name in French is *Médecins Sans Frontières*.

Humanitarian History

How Did the Red Cross Start?

In 1859, two armies fought a battle in a town in northern Italy. When the battle was over, thousands of wounded soldiers were left hurt or dying. No one helped them.

Henry Dunant

That night, Henry Dunant, a young Swiss man, was passing through the town. He was shocked to see so many wounded men with no one to care for them. He organized the townspeople to help him care for the soldiers.

Later, Dunant wrote a book about what he saw. He thought that groups of trained volunteers should help all people hurt because of war. Many people liked this idea. The Red Cross was formed in 1863.

How Did Amnesty International Start?

In 1960, Peter Benenson, an Englishman, read a newspaper article about two students in Portugal. The students had been put in jail because of their beliefs.

Peter Benenson

THE

SIX POLITICAL PRISONERS : le
a Rumanian gaol; centre, the Rev.
In gaol in the United States; right, A
without trial by the Portuguese. Th

ON BOTH SIDES of the
men and women are be
because their political o
those of their Governr
London lawyer, concei
campaign, APPEAL FOR
Governments to release
give them a fair trial. Th
and "The Observer" is g

The F

OPEN your newspaper any day of
the week and you will find a report
from somewhere in the world of
someone being imprisoned, tortured
or executed because his opinions or
religion are unacceptable to his
government. There are several
million such people in prison—by no
means all of them behind the Iron
and Bamboo Curtains—and their
numbers are growing. The newspaper reader feels a sickening sense
of impotence. Yet if these feelings of
disgust all over the world could be
united into common action, something effective could be done.

In 1945 the founder members of
the United Nations approved the
Universal Declaration of Human
Rights :—

Article 18.—Everyone has the right to
freedom of thought, conscience and
religion ; this right includes freedom
to change his religion or belief, and
freedom either alone or in com-
pany with others in public or private,
to manifest his religion or belief in
teaching practice, worship and
observance.

Article 19.—Everyone has the right to
freedom of opinion and expres-
sion ; this right includes freedom to
hold opinions without interference
and to seek, receive and impart
information and ideas through any
media and regardless

In 1961, Benenson started a **campaign** in a London newspaper. He wanted people to write letters of protest to governments that were holding prisoners unfairly.

Lots of people helped. Later that year, Amnesty International was formed.

BSERVER WEEKEND REVIEW

London, Sunday, May 28, 1961

21

Left, Archbishop Beran of Prague, held in custody by the Czechs; centre, Toni Ambatielos, the Greek Communist and trade unionist prisoner, whose wife is English; right Cardinal Mindszenty, Primate of Hungary, formerly a prisoner and now a political refugee trapped in the United States Embassy, Budapest.

...ca, the philosopher, now in ...end of the Negroes, recently ...golan poet and doctor, held ...cribed in the article below.

...in, thousands of ...gaol without trial ...iews differ from ...er Benenson, a ...ea of a world ..., 1961, to urge ...ple or at least ...n opens to-day, ...it a platform.

gotten Prisoners

...g tendency all ...guise the real ...non-conform-. In Spain, ...eaflets calling ...iscussions on ...harged with ..."I detest your ...In Hungary, ...ave tried to ...s open have ...osexuality." ...indicate that ...s means in-...of outside ...ld opinion ...weak spot, ...in making ...er instance, ...Dery was ...formation ...ttees" in ...Professor ...literary ...pain this ...some dis-

...mobilise ...widely, ...up in

campaign, which opens to-day, is the result of an initiative by a group of lawyers, writers and publishers in London, who share the underlying conviction expressed by Voltaire: "I detest your views, but am prepared to die for your right to express them." We have set up an office in London to collect information about the names, numbers and conditions of what we have decided to call "Prisoners of Conscience," and we define them thus: "Any person who is physically restrained (by imprisonment or otherwise) from expressing (in any form of words or symbols) any opinion which he honestly holds and which does not advocate or condone personal violence." We also exclude those who have conspired with a foreign government to overthrow their own. Our office will from time to time hold Press conferences to focus attention on Prisoners of Conscience selected impartially from different parts of the world. And it will provide factual information to any group, existing or new, in any part of the world, which decides to join in a special effort in favour of freedom of opinion or religion.

In October a Penguin Special called "Perse...

Amat, who tried to build a coalition of democratic groups, and has been in prison without trial since November, 1958; and of two white men persecuted by their own race for preaching that the coloured races should have equal rights—Ashton Jones, the sixty-five-year-old minister, who last year was repeatedly beaten-up and three times imprisoned in Louisiana and Texas for doing what the Freedom Riders are now doing in Alabama; and Patrick Duncan, the son of a former South African Governor-General, who, after three stays in prison, has just been served with an order forbidding him from attending or addressing any meeting for five years.

'Find out who is in gaol'

The technique of publicising the personal stories of a number of prisoners of contrasting politics is a new one. It has been adopted to avoid the fate of previous amnesty campaigns, which so often have become more concerned with publicising the political views of th...

out who is in gaol." This is hard advice to follow, because there are few governments which welcome inquiries about the number of Prisoners of Conscience they hold in prison. But another test of freedom one can apply is whether the Press is allowed to criticise the government. Even many democratic governments are surprisingly sensitive to Press criticism. In France, General de Gaulle has intensified newspaper seizures, a policy he inherited from the Fourth Republic. In Britain and the United States occasional attempts are made to draw the sting of Press criticism by the technique of taking editors into confidence about a "security secret," as in the Blake spy case.

Within the British Commonwealth, the Government of Ceylon has launched an attack on the Press, and is threatening to take the whole industry under public control. In Pakistan the Press is at the mercy of the Martial Law administration. In Ghana, the opposition Press operates under great disabilities. In South Afric...

lawyer is able to present the defence in the way he thinks best. In recent years there has been a regrettable trend in some of those countries that take pride in possessing an independent judiciary: by declaring a state of emergency and taking their opponents into "preventive detention," governments have side-stepped the need to make and prove criminal charges. At the other extreme there is the enthusiasm in Soviet countries to set up institutions which, though called courts, are really nothing of the sort. The so-called "comradely courts" in the U.S.S.R., which have power to deal with "parasites," are in essence little more than departments of the Ministry of Labour, shifting "square pegs" into empty holes in Siberia. In China the transmigration of labour by an allegedly judicial process is on a gigantic scale.

The most rapid way of bringing relief to Prisoners of Conscience is publicity, especially publicity among their fellow-citizens. With the pressure of emergent nationalism and the tensions of the Cold War, there are bound to be situations where governments are led to take emergency measures to protect their existence. It is vital that public opinion should insist that these measures should not be excessive, nor prolonged after the moment of danger. If the emergency is to last a long time, then a government should be induced to allow its opponents out of prison, to seek asylum abroad.

Frontier control more efficient

Although there are no statistics, it is likely that recent years have seen a steady decrease in the number of people reaching asylum. This is not so much due to the unwillingness of other countries to offer shelter, as to the greatly increased efficiency of frontier control, which to-day makes it harder for people to get away. Attempts to reach agree...

willing to give out translation and correspondence work to refugees, but no machinery to link supply with demand. Those regimes that refuse to allow their nationals to seek asylum on the ground that they go abroad only to conspire, might be less reluctant if they knew that, on arrival, the refugees would not be kicking their heels in idle frustration.

The members of the Council of Europe have agreed a Convention of Human Rights, and set up a commission to secure its enforcement. Some countries have accorded to their citizens the right to approach the commission individually. But some, including Britain, have refused to accept the jurisdiction of the commission over individual complaints, and France has refused to ratify the Convention at all. Public opinion should insist on the establishment of effective supra-national machinery not only in Europe but on similar lines in other continents.

This is an especially suitable year for an Amnesty Campaign. It is the centenary of President Lincoln's inauguration, and of the beginning of the Civil War which ended with the liberation of the American slaves; it is also the centenary of the decree that emancipated the Russian serfs. A hundred years ago Mr. Gladstone's budget swept away the oppressive duties on newsprint and so enlarged the range and freedom of the Press; 1861 marked the end of the tyranny of King "Bomba" of Naples, and the creation of a united Italy; it was also the year of the death of Lacordaire, the French Dominican opponent of Bourbon and Orleanist oppression.

The success of the 1961 Amnesty Campaign depends on how sharply and powerfully it is possible to rally public opinion. It depends, too, upon the campaign being all-embracing in its composition, international in character and politically impartial in direction. Any group is welcome to take part whic...

How Did Doctors Without Borders Start?

In 1971, a group of French doctors came together. Many of the doctors had worked in countries that had been in wars, or had been hit by disasters. These doctors believed all people had the right to medical aid. They started Doctors Without Borders.

The Nobel Peace Prize

Every year, the Nobel Peace Prize is given to a person, group, or organization that has done the most work to promote peace.

- Henry Dunant was given the prize in 1901.

- The Red Cross was given the prize in 1917, 1944, and 1963.

- Amnesty International was given the prize in 1977.

- Doctors Without Borders was given the prize in 1999.

One of the Doctors Without Borders workers accepting the Nobel Peace Prize.

Glossary

campaign organized actions with a purpose, such as helping people

famines when there is no food

gender whether you are male or female

humanitarian concerned with the well-being of all people

letters of protest letters written to people or governments about something that is wrong. People write letters of protest to try and get people or governments to change their actions.

organization an organized group of people

protests when people get together in a group to let other people or governments know that they are upset or angry about something.

race the ethnic group that people belong to

volunteers people who choose to work for no payment

wealth how much money and goods a person has

Index